Why We Assess Students — And How

T0312056

The Practicing Administrator's Leadership Series
Jerry J. Herman and Janice L. Herman, Editors

ROADMAPS
TO SUCCESS

Other Titles in This Series Include:

(see back cover for additional titles)

Why We Assess Students — And How

The Competing Measures of Student Performance

James E. McLean
Robert E. Lockwood

CORWIN PRESS, INC.
A Sage Publications Company
Thousand Oaks, California

For information address:

Corwin Press, Inc.
A Sage Publications Company
2455 Teller Road
Thousand Oaks, California 91320
e-mail: order@corwin.sagepub.com

SAGE Publications Ltd.
6 Bonhill Street
London EC2A 4PU
United Kingdom

SAGE Publications India Pvt. Ltd.
M-32 Market
Greater Kailash I
New Delhi 110 048 India

Printed in the United States of America

Library of Congress Cataloging-in-Publication Data

McLean, James E.
        Why we assess students—and how: the competing measures of student performance / James E. McLean, Robert E. Lockwood.
        p.   cm. — (Roadmaps to success)
        Includes bibliographical references.
        ISBN 0-8039-6335-1 (pbk. : alk. paper)
        1. Education tests and measurements—United States. 2. Academic achievement—United States—Evaluation.   I. Lockwood, Robert E., 1949-   . II. Title. III. Series.
        LB3051.M462495   1996
        371.2'6—dc20   96-44371

This book is printed on acid-free paper.

96 97 98 99 00 10 9 8 7 6 5 4 3 2 1

Corwin Press Production Editor: S. Marlene Head

Contents

Foreword

James McLean and Robert Lockwood have applied their extensive expertise in the area of assessment in an easily read, short, and powerful book titled *Why We Assess Students—And How: The Competing Measures of Student Performance.* In five chapters, they summarize the types of assessments, the strengths and weaknesses of each type, the proper uses of assessment data, and the cautions to be observed when administering, securing, and interpreting assessment results. Chapter 1 discusses the current arguments for and against the various methods of assessment, the quality requirements for test instruments, and the need to pay attention to equity and test bias issues. Chapter 2 addresses the development, administration, uses, and interpretation of norm-referenced testing and discusses its strengths and weaknesses.

Similar discussions of criterion-referenced testing and alternative or authentic testing methodologies are found in chapters 3 and 4. Chapter 5 demonstrates how to develop an ideal assessment program for your school or school system.

This book is a keeper. Put it on your desk and use it frequently!

JERRY J. HERMAN
JANICE L. HERMAN
Series Co-Editors

Preface

Every school administrator and teacher must deal with assessments and assessment results. Whether it is giving the tests, using the results, or explaining their meaning to parents or board members, assessment is an essential part of the job. This book attempts to demystify that process by taking a commonsense approach.

The book addresses the roles assessments play in education, and it provides detailed descriptions of norm-referenced tests, criterion-referenced tests, and alternative assessment strategies, along with their appropriate and inappropriate applications. The book also provides guidelines on reducing bias and dealing with special populations. The last chapter provides an example of an ideal assessment program and the steps needed to establish one in any school system.

We wish to express our appreciation to several people who made this publication possible. First, we appreciate Jerry Herman's asking us to submit a proposal and for making sure we stayed on schedule. We also appreciate his and Janice Herman's (co-editors of the Roadmaps to Success series) many fine suggestions. We hope we have done them justice. We wish to express our appreciation to the people at Corwin Press, including Gracia Alkema, Ann

McMartin, and others in the production end of the process. We are especially appreciative to Michele Jarrell who developed Figure 2.1 on the computer to our exacting specifications. This figure was a real roadblock in the project. Thanks to Anna Williams and Anne Lockwood for several proofreadings of the manuscript. Finally, we appreciate the cooperation of our families, who allowed us to spend the time away from them to complete the writing.

JAMES E. MCLEAN
ROBERT E. LOCKWOOD

About the Authors

James E. McLean has worked with teachers, administrators, and state educational officials on assessment issues for more than 21 years. His formal education includes a Ph.D. in the foundations of education, a master's degree in statistics, and a B.S. in education from the University of Florida. He currently serves as a University Research Professor and Director of Research in the School of Education at the University of Alabama at Birmingham, where he is developing a research center for the school. For the past 26 years, he has taught, researched, and administered programs including the direction, codirection, or administration of more than 100 research, assessment, and evaluation projects. Most of these projects have been conducted in public schools. McLean has received the two highest teaching awards given by the University of Alabama—the National Alumni Association Outstanding Commitment to Teaching Award (1991) and the Burlington Northern Foundation Faculty Achievement Award in Teaching (1989). His research has been recognized by the American Educational Research Association (1981 Division H Award for the Best Report of an Evaluation Study), the Mensa Education and Research Foundation (1988-1989 Award for Excellence in Research), and the Mid-South Educational Research Association (Outstanding Research

Paper Awards in 1988, 1993, and 1994). His students have won numerous awards for their research.

Robert E. Lockwood received his Ph.D. in educational psychology and research and a master's degree in educational psychology from the University of Alabama. He also holds a B.S. in psychology from Troy State University. His graduate training included statistics, measurement, administration, and educational evaluation. He is currently Supervisor of the Office of Assessment for the Alabama State Department of Education, where he has worked for the past 12 years. He also holds adjunct faculty appointments with the University of Alabama and Auburn University at Montgomery, where he teaches courses in quantitative methods and educational psychology. Prior to joining the State Department of Education, Lockwood worked with the American College Testing Program and the Educational Testing Service in the area of certification and licensure examinations. He has also worked with the Army Research Institute to design a revised Flight Aptitude Selection Test used to select applicants for helicopter flight training. His areas of research interest include standard setting, applied research in schools, and student assessment.

The Role of Assessment
in Education

S tudent testing has been part of the educational enterprise since its inception. Every day, millions of students take tests, most of which are designed and administered by classroom teachers to see how well their students have learned what the teacher has taught and sometimes to evaluate the instructional program. The process of giving tests and using their results is referred to as assessment. These tests may range from 5-minute quizzes to multi-day end-of-year examinations. Test forms may be multiple-choice, fill-in-the-blank, book report, oral presentation, essay, or an actual demonstration of skills (such as a science experiment). Classroom tests usually have one or more of the following purposes:

- To see how well a student has learned a specific lesson
- To determine each student's strengths and weaknesses so that instruction can be directed to appropriate areas
- To determine a student's grades for reporting purposes
- To measure a student's progress over time

It is important to remember that a classroom test is unique to a particular teacher and class. The results are not meant to be

1

compared with students' work in other classes. However, the results are useful to the teacher and to the student when directed toward improving learning.

There is another category of test, however, that is not designed by the teacher. These tests are designed by professional test publishers for use in schools and classrooms nationwide. These tests are referred to as norm-referenced tests because their results are reported in terms of how students perform with respect to a comparison group. This type of test uses standardized rules and procedures for administration and scoring, but they also cause the most confusion among teachers, school administrators, and parents. Educators, parents, policymakers, and taxpayers use these tests not only to measure progress in the classroom but also for purposes such as measuring school accountability or for assuring equality of educational opportunity.

These tests are often inadequately referred to as "standardized tests," and they are designed to provide information to people beyond classroom teachers and school administrators. They have been used as criteria for eligibility for admission to, as well as the evaluation of, special school programs such as Title I or gifted education. Students' scores are often aggregated to monitor and describe performance of classrooms, schools, school systems, and states. At the local level, they are sometimes used to analyze the progress of student subgroups. Standardized tests are administered and scored under the same conditions for all students. Although most people associate standardized tests with multiple-choice, norm-referenced tests, it is important to realize that standardization is a concept that is applicable for any testing format or test type, including those that are not norm referenced, such as writing assessments and oral presentations. For example, any state that has a graduation test as a requirement for receiving a high school diploma will go to great lengths to assure that all students take the test under the same conditions and that the tests are scored and reported in a comparable fashion. In other words, care is taken to make sure that all students have a fair and equal chance to demonstrate that their achievement meets the state's criteria as worthy of a diploma. The "standardization" aspect of standardized testing refers to the conditions under which the test was given and scored, not the type of test nor the type of scores reported.

Current Conflict About Assessment

The educational reform efforts of the past 10 years largely have been driven by assessment and assessment results. Merely increasing the funding for schools or adding programs no longer satisfies parents or the general public who pays for education. The public, through elected officials, is demanding that the effectiveness of changes in schools be demonstrated by increases in student performance. Even though the original purpose of student assessment was to assist classroom teachers in improving student instruction by measuring what students were taught, it is now seen by the public as a means of accountability for the entire educational system. The primary purposes of assessment, instructional improvement and educational accountability, often are seen to be in conflict with one another. On one hand, teachers are demanding better data on which to base instructional decisions about students. On the other hand, parents, school boards, and the general public are demanding data that compare the performance of children with those of the entire state, nation, or the world. A truly effective comprehensive assessment program must address both of these broad purposes.

These two purposes for assessment generally are addressed using two different types of assessment instruments or tests: nationally norm-referenced tests and criterion-referenced tests. Nationally standardized norm-referenced tests are developed by giving the test to a nationally representative sample of students and computing standard scores that report how each student performed with respect to that national norm group. For example, percentile ranks are the most common standard scores reported, and a percentile rank represents the percentage of students in the norming population who performed at or below the level of that particular student. On the other hand, criterion-referenced tests measure the content of a specific curriculum, and the scores that are reported represent how well a student has mastered that curriculum. The results from criterion-referenced tests are often reported in terms of the percentage of items answered correctly or as achievement levels that are compared with a predetermined "cut score."

To illustrate the differences between norm-referenced tests and criterion-referenced tests, consider a program designed to improve the height that students can attain when performing the high jump. A norm-referenced method of testing would provide information about how high each student jumped relative to some norming population. For example, we might find that Johnny can jump as high or higher than 38% of that population. However, this does not tell the coach specifically how high he can jump, whether Johnny is jumping to his capacity, or if Johnny is showing improvement. An alternative method of assessment would be to set instructional goals (i.e., a criterion or standard) and assess whether the students meet these goals. The goals would be in terms of the height jumped. The coach would get a baseline on which to design and plan an instructional program, and she would further use these data to determine if the instructional goals have been met. This approach, criterion-referenced testing, could be used to assess improvement and, consequently, the instructional techniques employed by the coach.

As previously noted, the two primary purposes of an assessment program are often seen to be in conflict with one another. Many taxpayers and politicians feel that nationally standardized norm-referenced tests are necessary for accountability purposes, whereas many educators suggest that norm-referenced tests do not provide information relevant to what their particular students were taught. Many educators favor criterion-referenced tests that provide them with relevant information for making instructional decisions about their curriculum. Although both norm-referenced tests and criterion-referenced tests have their strengths and weaknesses, a comprehensive assessment program must embrace both types of tests.

Norm-referenced tests are neither as effective and accurate as their supporters believe, nor as error-ridden and useless as their detractors allege. As with any tests, they have their own strengths and weaknesses. Although they provide an excellent basis for comparing groups of students, they primarily measure memorized knowledge and understanding, and they generally fail to provide clear insight into the application of knowledge. Their "normative" results are often misleading because the norms may be out of date or misinterpreted, the level of adherence to the standardized administration conditions may not have been adequate for all test administrations, or there may be disparities between the state's educational objectives and those on which the test was based. However, norm-referenced tests do provide general information about how well students are performing on a common, nationally recognized set of skills, and when applied longitudinally, normative test data can provide evidence of learning.

Criterion-referenced tests meet educators' needs for instructional guidance by providing information targeted to specific instructional objectives. However, the public is often concerned that the criteria are not rigorous enough because they may have been based on minimal levels of achievement. Although this may be true for some assessments, the criteria can be set to reflect any level of expectation. In fact, multiple criteria may be set on the same criterion-referenced assessments, such as the levels of writing proficiency from statewide writing tests. The ability to provide a national comparison is lost, but statewide comparisons can be implemented. Criterion-referenced tests can assess students' abilities to apply skills, such as problem solving, and they are designed to be highly similar to classroom instructional activities.

Recent education literature has promoted the value of alternative assessments such as "performance assessments" or "authentic assessments." Although application of these types of assessment is relatively new for large-scale and standardized testing, they have been used commonly in classrooms for decades. Science experiments, student projects, and student essays are examples of performance assessments. Performance assessments are most often criterion referenced but they may be norm referenced. An excellent example of a performance assessment is the part of the driving test where the applicant drives a car over a course performing specified maneuvers and is rated by an examiner. It is criterion referenced in the sense that the maneuvers are chosen in terms of what a driver will face on public roads, and a minimum level of performance is specified under the assumption that a driver meeting this level of performance would not be a danger on the road.

The Quality of Tests

The overall quality of a test is usually measured in terms of the test's validity and reliability. Although a detailed discussion of validity and reliability is beyond the scope of this book, a brief description of these concepts is important to the understanding of their role in the selection of assessment instruments.

The validity of a test is the level to which the test measures what it is supposed to measure. Thus the validity of a test depends on the purpose for its use. Test developers use various terms to describe types of test validity (e.g., content, concurrent, predictive, and construct validity). However, for most school programs, test validity depends on the degree to which the content of the test and the method used to measure that content correspond to the content of the curriculum and the methods used for teaching. In a broad sense, this is content validity. It should be emphasized that a test may not be valid for all purposes but must be valid for the purpose for which it is being used.

Reliability is the consistency with which a test measures whatever it is measuring. A test could be very reliable, that is, a similar score is obtained in repeated uses, and still not be valid for its intended purpose. For example, having students step on a scale and obtaining their weights would be very reliable but may not produce valid measures of weight if the scale had not been properly calibrated before its use. A test cannot be valid without first being reliable. Reliability is usually indexed with a decimal fraction that ranges from .00 to 1.00. The larger the index, the less error present in the measurement. A simple rule of thumb to use would be to use tests with reliabilities of .70 or higher for making group decisions and .90 or higher for making individual decisions. Reliabilities generally are reported in a test's technical manuals.

Equal Opportunities for All Students

Potential testing bias against certain populations continues to be a major concern of educators. The Civil Rights movement following the Supreme Court decision on school desegregation in 1954 focused attention on the fairness of tests for African American and other minority populations. The Education for All Handicapped Children Act of 1975 (Public Law 94-142) and the Individuals with Disabilities Education Act of 1990 (IDEA), along with subsequent legislation and court actions, focused attention on the fairness of tests for exceptional children. The equality and fairness of the tests for all children must be considered in any assessment program.

Testing Bias

A test is considered biased if students' scores depend on something other than what is being tested. For example, consider a question on a test that requires the person to calculate the score in a football game using the following information: The Colts scored two touchdowns and two field goals and the Dolphins scored three touchdowns and no field goals. What was the final score of the game? A person who did not know the rules of American football would probably get the item wrong, even if he or she was excellent in mathematical calculation. We usually think of tests as biased when the members of a minority group do not perform as well as others or when girls do not perform as well as boys. Although both of these situations may be due to biased tests, it is not necessarily true. In many such situations, the bias can be traced to the instruction or a lack of equality of learning opportunities rather than to the tests themselves. For example, suppose that an item on an elementary school mathematics achievement test is "$38 \times 76 = $ ___," and two groups perform quite differently on the item. Is the item biased? Although that is possible, it is very unlikely. If we assume that the groups are of equal ability, the difference can often be traced to differences in opportunities to learn. Therefore, differences in test performance do not necessarily translate into test bias.

Although differential test performance is not prima facie evidence that a test is biased, it does mean that the test may have an "adverse impact." In some other uses of testing, such as for employment, there are legal requirements relating to a test's potential adverse impact. In education, we try to reduce the adverse impact to the extent possible by equalizing every student's opportunity to learn. The major problem in determining test bias is separating the parts of differential performance that are due to test bias from differences that are due to other causes. A popular approach is to identify groups of students with similar characteristics based on ability, socioeconomic background, or prior achievement and then compare the performance of these groups with each other. Differences in test performance among these otherwise homogeneous groups are then more likely to be due to test bias.

Unless an administrator is going to pay to have all tests custom developed, there are limited actions that can be taken to minimize test bias. Probably, the most useful approach begins with the selection of tests. Data are usually available on differential group performance. If not, small pilot testing can be done. Another useful tool that should not be overlooked is the use of bias committees to review tests and test items before a test is adopted. It should be noted that the more content-valid a test is (i.e., the more a test reflects the curriculum being tested), the less likely it is to be biased. Bias committees that include members of groups the test may be biased against can provide valuable information about test bias. When these steps are taken, data on adverse impact should still be collected with an eye toward minimizing it in the future.

Testing of Special Education Students

Test bias is also a concern when testing special education students. However, it is only one of the things that must be considered. With special education students, test bias is often quite subtle and is related to specific handicapping conditions. For example, suppose that an item on a high school achievement test uses "driving a car" to illustrate the concept. A nonsighted person may be at a disadvantage on such an item because it would be beyond his or her experience even if that person totally understands the concept.

The most troublesome testing issue for many educators relating to the testing of special education students concerns what, if any, accommodations should be provided. An accommodation is an environmental adaptation made to negate, to the extent possible without altering the integrity of the test and test scores, the impact of an individual's disability on his or her test performance. The term was originally proposed by Jean Piaget, a well-known French developmental psychologist. An example of an appropriate accommodation is the reading of a mathematics test to a dyslexic student. The real question is when and if an accommodation should be provided. Unfortunately, the answer is not simple. It depends on a number of factors. Probably, the primary factor among them is the content of the student's Individual Educational Plan (IEP). If having material read to the student is included in the student's normal accommodations, most tests should be read to the student. Even this is not absolute. For example, what if a student's IEP specifies that material is to be read to the student, but the test in question is a high school graduation examination that includes a reading portion that must be passed to receive a high school diploma? Should the reading examination be read to the student? Although this question must be answered on an individual basis, it should be recognized that any accommodation changes the specific competencies that are being measured by the test. Test accommodations can also have a dramatic effect on test norms. This aspect of applying accommodations is discussed in more detail in chapter 2.

The bottom line is that legal and logical principles must be applied to decisions regarding accommodations. For example, even though a nonsighted individual may be able to work the gas and brake pedals, steer a car, and give signals if someone were in the car to give directions, this accommodation for a driving test probably should not be provided.

Summary

Assessment is the process of giving tests and using their results. The types of tests that are used affect the types of decisions we can make. The most popular types of tests are norm-referenced tests and criterion-referenced tests. These tests are often seen to be in conflict with one another. Nationally standardized norm-referenced tests are best suited for comparing student performance on a national basis, and they are often preferred by the general public because they are suited for making accountability decisions. Criterion-referenced tests compare student performance to established criteria, often based on the local curricula, and they are preferred by educators because they are suited for making educational decisions. A well-balanced assessment program will include both types of tests.

Norm-Referenced Assessment

As noted in chapter 1, traditional norm-referenced tests are often incompletely referred to as standardized tests. Although any test can be given, scored, and reported under standardized conditions (making it a "standardized test"), this feature is most closely associated with norm-referenced tests. Norm-referenced tests have the added feature that the results can be reported in terms of one or more norming groups. The norms can provide additional meaning to the scores. However, norm-referenced scores can also easily be misinterpreted.

Reporting Norm-Referenced Results

One advantage ascribed to norm-referenced tests is that their results can be reported in terms of how an individual student performs relative to an identified norming group. This is done by transforming the raw scores (number of items answered correctly) of students into what are called standard scores. To discuss standard scores, it is necessary to provide a brief description of three descriptive statistics—mean, median, and standard deviation.

The mean and median are representations of the middle of a set of scores. The mean is the arithmetic average of a set of scores. This statistic is used by most teachers to determine summary grades at the end of each grading period. The median, on the other hand, represents the middle point of a set of scores. It is the point in a set of scores where exactly one half of the scores are smaller and one half are larger. If a set of scores is symmetrical (the upper and lower halves of the score distribution mirror each other), the mean and median will be the same value. Otherwise, the mean will be closer to the end of the distribution with the more extreme values.

Whereas the mean and median describe the center of a set of data, the standard deviation describes its variability. The value of a standard deviation can range from 0.00 to any positive number. A typical large set of data will cover about six standard deviations with about two thirds of the scores falling in the middle two standard deviations. About 95% of the scores will fall in the middle four standard deviations, and almost all of the scores will fall in the middle six standard deviations. Scores beyond the six-standard-deviations range are often referred to as outliers because they do not fit the typical distributional properties of the data.

With these brief descriptions of mean, median, and standard deviation in mind, some of the more common standard scores are as follows.

Percentile rank. A student's percentile rank indicates the percentage of students in the norming group who scored less than or equal to that student's score. The median score in the norming group is the 50th percentile; half the scores are above and half are below. For example, if Anne scored at the 64th percentile, she scored as well or better than 64% of the norming group.

Stanine scores. Sometimes, scores are reported in categories. The most common example is the nine-category score scale called a "stanine scale" that has a middle category of five. The so-called stanine scale derives its name from the words *stan*dard *nine*. It is constructed by converting the raw scores to a scale with a mean of 5 and a standard deviation of 2 and rounding to the nearest whole number. Extreme values below 1 and above 9 are converted to 1 and 9, respectively.

Linear standard scores. Linear standard scores are raw scores transformed to a standard scale with a specified mean and standard deviation. Common examples are z scores (mean of 0.0 and standard deviation of 1.0), T scores (mean of 50 and standard deviation of 10), and Wechsler IQ scores (mean of 100 and standard deviation of 15).

Grade equivalent scores. Grade equivalent scores are devised using multiple norming groups and indicate the estimated grade (in a year.month format) corresponding to the student's performance. For example, a test intended for fifth-grade students may be normed by giving it to fifth graders at the beginning of the year and at the end of the year, fourth graders at the beginning and end of the year, and sixth graders at the beginning and end of the year. The mean scores of each of these groups are computed, and these become the raw scores equivalent to the grade equivalent scores, which, in turn, become the norms for those time periods. For example, suppose fifth graders in the 1st month of the year averaged 38 raw score points and fifth graders in the 9th month averaged 56 points. A raw score of 38 would translate to a grade equivalent score of 5.1 and a raw score of 56 would translate to a grade equivalent score of 5.9. The scores in between are estimated linearly. For example, a raw score of 42 would be translated to a grade equivalent score of 5.3 because it is the same proportional distance between 5.1 and 5.9 as 42 is between 38 and 56. Raw scores less than and greater than the norming group means are also determined by estimating linearly, a process called extrapolation.

Scaled scores. Scaled scores are developed by test publishers to compare results across different levels of a test. For example, an achievement battery developed for kindergarten through 12th grade might have scaled scores that range from 200 through 800. Supposedly, a 300 earned by a fourth-grade student means the same as a 300 earned by a fifth-grade student. Scaled scores are used primarily for analyses that involve multiple levels of the test.

Normal curve equivalents (NCEs). The NCE scale is a special case of the linear standard score scale that is based on percentiles. NCEs range from 1 to 99, with a mean (and median) of 50. In fact, NCEs 1, 50, and 99 correspond exactly to the 1st, 50th, and 99th percentiles, respectively. The other NCEs are equally spaced between those percentiles. The result is a standard score scale with a mean of 50 and a standard deviation of 21.06. Figure 2.1 depicts a normally shaped distribution of data with standard deviations and some common standard scores.

Selecting a Standard Score Scale

Each of the standard scores described in the previous section has its advantages and disadvantages. Percentile ranks are easily explained to parents and other test consumers. However, they are often confused with percentage-correct raw scores. Linear standard scores such as z scores, T scores, and NCEs are useful for performing statistical analyses because they have equal numerical intervals. However, they generally have little meaning for most teachers, school administrators, and parents.

Grade equivalent scores are misleadingly self-explanatory. That is, they provide a false impression of their meaning. For example, many people would interpret a 6.6 grade equivalent score earned by a fourth student to mean that the student scored well into the sixth-grade level, and they may infer that the student should be placed into the sixth grade. It must be emphasized that the 6.6 grade equivalent really means that it is estimated that the student scored as well as a sixth-grade student would score on fourth-grade material (because the fourth-grade test did not include sixth-grade material). Concepts introduced between the fourth and sixth grades are not likely to have been on the test and were not tested. Considering methods used for estimating grade equivalent scores for grades other than those tested in the norming group and their susceptibility to misinterpretation, we recommend that *grade equivalent scores not be used for any purpose or even reported.*

Stanine scores have the advantage of not overly classifying students. With only nine categories, student performance can be

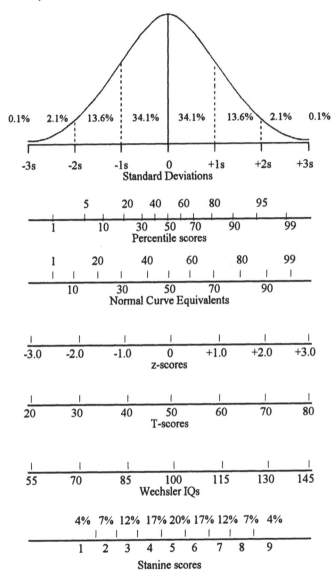

Figure 2.1. Common Standard Score Scales and Percentages

reported in broad categories. These categories are often grouped further. Stanines 1-3 are considered "below average," stanines 4-6 are considered "average," and stanines 7-9 are considered "above average."

Our recommendation is to report percentile ranks, stanine scores, or both when reporting the results of a nationally standardized norm-referenced test. Grade equivalent scores should not be used or reported because they are susceptible to misinterpretation. Other standard scores such as z scores, T scores, Wechsler IQ scores, and scaled scores (including NCEs) should be reserved for those special tests that have traditionally used these scores and for research purposes. In those situations, they are usually interpreted by people trained in their use, such as school psychologists and researchers. Regardless of which score scale is used to report the results, the norming group on which it is based must be kept in mind. A more detailed discussion of this is in the next section.

Norming Groups and Interpretation

No standardized test score can be interpreted properly without carefully considering the norming group on which its standard scores are based. Not only is a description of the norming group important, but other factors such as the date the test was normed and the conditions used during the norming must be considered. In chapter 1, it was noted that accommodations for special education students would change the interpretation of the standard scores reported. The fact is that any deviation from the original conditions used when the test was normed changes the interpretation of the standard scores.

To illustrate this point, consider an application of the Algebraic Achievement Test (AAT), a test designed to measure the content of a high school Algebra 1 course. (Note: This is a fictitious test.) Suppose there were 180 possible points on the AAT. Regina, a ninth-grade student who just completed Algebra 1, took the AAT and achieved 110 raw score points. As it turned out, the AAT was normed several times, and Regina's performance could be compared to each of these groups. If Regina's percentile score was reported, comparing her performance to each of these norming groups, her percentile rank would vary depending on the norm group. Specifically, she scored equal to or better than

- 22% of students who completed college algebra at a major university
- 38% of students who completed college algebra at a community college
- 45% of students who completed Algebra 2 in high school
- 48% of ninth-grade students who completed Algebra 1 this past year and took the test under the same standard conditions as the norming group
- 55% of ninth-grade students completing Algebra 1 this past year who took the test without time limits
- 72% of ninth-grade students who completed Algebra 1 ten years earlier
- 98% of seventh-grade students who just completed general math

The fact that Regina's raw score of 110 resulted in percentile scores as low as 22 and as high as 98 illustrates the importance of considering the norming group. Not only is the norming group itself important, but the age of the norms and the conditions under which the test was taken can also influence the results. Although Regina's raw score remained 110, her percentile rank varied from 22 to 98, depending on the norming group, age of the norms, and the norming conditions.

Research has demonstrated that test norms become less and less accurate when a test is used over a long period of time, particularly if the test is not kept under secure conditions. As students and teachers become familiar with what is on the test, the curriculum slowly changes to reflect the content of the test and the students' norm-referenced scores improve. Some have referred to this as the "Lake Wobegon effect," named for the mythical town referred to by Garrison Keillor in his popular radio show, the Prairie Home Companion, where "all the women are strong, all the men are good-looking, and all the children are above average."

Summary

A norm-referenced test is a test that provides information relative to an identified norming group. An individual score can only be interpreted in relation to the norm group. To interpret a score properly, one must have knowledge of the norm group and the particular score scale that is being used. Nationally, standardized norm-referenced tests are particularly popular with the public and elected officials because they are used for accountability purposes.

Criterion-Referenced
Assessment

The difference between a norm-referenced test and a criterion-referenced test is not something that can be learned by looking at the test itself. The items on a norm-referenced test may be identical to the items on a criterion-referenced test in the same subject. The debate over these two types of tests is really a debate over how student performance is reported and how these scores may be used. The choice of which test is best for any situation comes back, as it always does, to the purpose for giving the test. The purpose for giving a test will guide the selection of the type of test to be used in a particular situation. If the purpose is to compare performance with some other group, then the type of score that is needed is a norm-referenced score. If, on the other hand, the purpose of the test, from a simple quiz to a final examination, is to find out what students know and have learned from specific instruction, then the type of score we are looking for is a criterion-referenced score.

In chapter 2, we learned that a norm-referenced score compares a particular student's achievement to the achievement of a large group of students who took the same test under similar conditions at some time in the past. It does not tell us much about whether the student mastered our course of study or learned concepts we tried to teach. It did, however, tell us whether the achievement was above or below the average achievement of the norm group, with some measure of how far above or below that average the score fell. In this chapter, we discuss the situation where the teacher, administrator, or policymaker (public) wants to know how well a student has learned specific knowledge and skills from a well-defined content area. The need for this type of information may be found in requirements for promotion, planning instruction, remediation, awarding grades, or certifying the acquisition of knowledge. The type of test needed to answer these questions is a criterion-referenced test, and the type of score needed is a criterion-referenced score. According to Popham (1990), a criterion-referenced test is used to ascertain a student's status with respect to a well-defined assessment domain, or simply to determine what a student knows or does not know.

A criterion-referenced test is developed so that it may be used to report how a student's performance on the test reflects the student's knowledge of the content area being assessed. There are a great number of situations in which we may need to know what the student knows. At the beginning of school, a teacher may want to evaluate the initial knowledge level of students as a baseline for instruction; the state may want to ascertain the knowledge of driving rules and laws before awarding a driver's license; and a medical association may want to evaluate a physician's knowledge before awarding certification to the doctor. Regardless of the particular application, in some way we need to determine whether the student (or other individual) has the desired level of knowledge of the subject area for our purposes.

Purposes of Criterion-Referenced Tests

One of the clearest examples of a criterion-referenced test, already mentioned, is the knowledge and performance test given to driver's license applicants. The purpose is to assure safety on the highways. The knowledge test is developed to determine if the person has enough knowledge of driving rules, laws, and procedures to be allowed to drive on the highways of the state. The state has an interest in whether the knowledge level demonstrated on the test is high enough to justify the assumption that the person has acquired the knowledge needed to be a safe driver and whether other drivers can make that same assumption. Will the new driver know to signal a left turn prior to making the turn? Is it safe to assume that the person will not turn left from the right lane? Is it safe to assume that the person understands the meaning of a yield sign? These are important questions, and the answers are critical for assuring some measure of safety on the highway. Merely comparing someone's score on the driver's license test to a group of people who took the test a few years back and finding out the score was at the 70th percentile will not give the state or other drivers the same confidence as knowing that the person has met minimum criteria, i.e., scored high enough to pass the test. When someone passes the test, the inference the state and all other drivers make is that the person knows enough to be a safe driver.

In an instructional setting, there are many possible reasons for needing and using criterion-referenced tests. Within a classroom, these reasons might include diagnosing a student's weaknesses in a particular subject area so as to plan remedial instruction, gathering information to use for assigning grades to students, or using it as a pretest for an instructional unit to assess the degree of knowledge prior to teaching the instructional unit. At the school or system level, the test might be used to measure whether the scope and sequence for the particular curriculum is being fully implemented or to evaluate the instructional programs in areas such as Title I, Tech Prep, or Effective Schools. At the state level, the reasons might include assessing the implementation of the state courses of study or as part of an accountability system such as a high school exit examination.

Regardless of whether the criterion-referenced test is being used to test drivers or to test knowledge of a science unit, the purpose is the same—to assess knowledge against an established criterion or domain of desired knowledge. The purpose of the test is to obtain information about learning so that a decision may be made about whether the examinee has the specified level of knowledge of the content area.

Achievement Levels

Many criterion-referenced tests in education are designed to yield a simple pass or fail classification. To determine these two categories requires that a single cut score (sometimes called the passing score or a standard) be established on the test. There are many methods used to set this cut score, but virtually all of them involve identifying the test score that allows someone to infer that the student has "passed" the test. Even though this is the most common application, many tests being used today are designed to yield multiple classifications.

The classifications are usually referred to as achievement levels and may be described with words such as *novice, adequate, proficient,* and *superior.* The National Assessment of Educational Progress (NAEP) reports four classifications (*below basic, basic, proficient,* and *advanced*). Other states or applications may report three achievement levels, and some programs report as many as six achievement levels. The number of cut scores needed to establish achievement classifications is always one less than the number of classifications desired. Thus, to establish four classifications from a single test would require three cut scores. These three scores would separate each of the achievement levels. For example, three cut scores would need to be established to separate Level 1 from Level 2, Level 2 from Level 3, and Level 3 from Level 4.

The recent introduction of achievement levels in reporting the results of large-scale assessments (usually interpreted to mean state-level programs) has led some to believe that this is a new way of reporting student performance. In fact, this method of reporting is most familiar for reporting test performance to schoolchildren. During most people's schooling, the teacher graded all papers and tests using four cut scores—one to separate the As from the Bs, one to separate the Bs from the Cs, one to separate the Cs from the Ds, and one to indicate failure or F. It is the application of this method to large-scale assessments outside the classroom that is new. The use of this type of reporting for criterion-referenced tests gives different information about student achievement than an average score.

Establishing Cut Scores

Criterion-referenced tests are developed so that teachers and others may estimate the degree of learning by students in a particular subject area. The question of interest is: "Does the level of performance on the test justify the conclusion that the subject domain has been learned?" This question implies that a standard of performance exists. This performance standard often is referred to as a cut score. The establishment of a cut score involves deciding what level of performance represents acceptable evidence that the subject domain has been learned. This decision can only be made by those who are most knowledgeable of both the subject area of interest and of the performance of those who are taking the test. In schools, these people are the teachers.

In a classroom, the cut score used to determine who will pass a teacher's test is set by the teacher and often is no more complex than stating that 70% of the items answered correctly is passing. This type of standard setting has occurred since the earliest days of education. Until recently, however, this process has been a relatively subjective activity undertaken by the teacher on an "as needed" basis. With the increasingly high stakes attached to test performance, such as passing a graduation examination to receive a high school diploma, more objective, structured methods for determining cut scores were needed. The students themselves have to be assured that the cut score is valid, and the public must view the cut score as reasonable for the purpose intended. For example, the passing score on a high school graduation test must be high enough to be useful in identifying those worthy of a diploma but not so high that few can obtain that score.

The various standard setting or cut score procedures are based on the informed judgment of teachers or other experts. The difference between standard setting in the classroom and these procedures is the involvement of more than one teacher and the structured nature of these procedures. The various standard setting methods may be classified based on the type of judgments being made by the teachers. There is one group of procedures that requires the teacher to make judgments about the difficulty of the items on the test (e.g., the Angoff and Nedelsky procedures), and there is a second group that requires the teachers to make judgments about the level of competence of the students before testing and then to evaluate the performance of these students on the actual test (e.g., the contrasting-groups and borderline-groups procedures). A recent variation of the judgments about the students used in evaluating writing assessments has been for judges to review student papers and to classify the levels of performance of the papers as a method for determining the cut scores between levels of performance.

For methods that require judgments about the items (e.g., Angoff and Nedelsky), the judges are asked to estimate the difficulty of the items for the type of students who meet the criteria and for those who do not meet the criteria. For example, if the test in question is a high school graduation examination, the judges might be asked about their estimates of how difficult the item would be for students who have just barely mastered the knowledge required to receive a high school diploma. The judges continue on an item-by-item basis estimating item difficulties, and usually the sum of all the item difficulties on the test is the cut score.

The methods that require a judgment about the student (e.g., the contrasting-groups and borderline-groups procedures) ask the judges to estimate whether each particular student meets the knowledge expectation to pass. These judgments are used to classify the students into groups, and the average scores on the test for the groups are used to set the cut score. For example, the average test score for a group of students classified as borderline (in terms of the knowledge required) would be defined as the cut score. Using the contrasting-groups method, a score between an obvious mastery group (as judged by the teacher) and nonmastery group would be the cut score.

Of all the proposed procedures for establishing cut scores, the most common in practice is the one proposed by Angoff. This procedure is relatively easy for judges to understand and implement, and it has been applied in many different situations. It is applicable to multiple-choice items as well as to open-ended items. To gain a deeper understanding of the general concepts of standard setting using an Angoff-type procedure, the following example is provided.

Assume that a school system wants to establish some cut scores on an Algebra 1 examination so that the system can identify students who perform at a level that would qualify them to enroll in an advanced mathematics program. The system needs to establish a single cut score to separate this group of superior mathematics students from the merely "good" students. Although the process could be used to set three, four, or more cut scores, our example is limited to one cut score. For the purposes of this example, suppose that the Algebra 1 examination has only 10 items composed of both multiple-choice and open-ended items. The items on the test represent the full range of the course content, and therefore the test contains relatively easy items and relatively difficult items.

The first step in the process is to provide training and directions for the judges. In this example, we will assume that there are seven mathematics teachers from the high schools who can serve as judges. The judges are introduced to the task by explaining the purpose of the standard-setting process. In this case, the system wants to identify students qualified for this advanced mathematics program. Following this introduction, the judges discuss the level of achievement necessary for students to qualify for this program. They try to reach a consensus about the level of achievement and picture such a student in their minds. These mathematics teachers probably have taught the type of student being sought. Guided discussion among the judges helps them to picture the "typical" student meeting the expectations.

The second step is to evaluate each item on the test in terms of what proportion of these ideal students should be able to answer the item correctly. A useful method for doing this is for each judge to picture 100 of these typical students in their minds and answer the question, "How many of these students will answer the item correctly?" By adding a decimal point, the results from this process can easily be converted to proportions. These estimates for each item would be averaged across the seven judges to arrive at an estimated item difficulty for each item.

The third step is for the judges to reconsider their individual item estimates in light of information from a pilot administration of the test, the aggregated estimates from all the judges, or both. If a judge feels that his or her estimate is too high or too low based on this empirical evidence, it can be modified. For example, if all judges except one had estimates between .5 and .6 and one judge had estimated the difficulty to be .9, that judge could reconsider the estimate or, possibly, convince the other judges that it was appropriate. It is important to point out that no adjustment is required; only the opportunity to revise is provided.

After each judge has had the opportunity to revise the original item estimates, the estimates are averaged over the judges for each item. The cut score for the test is the sum of the average item estimates. Table 3.1 demonstrates this process for the example. It can be seen from Table 3.1 that the sum of the difficulty estimates is 6.64. Thus the cut score would be 6.64 items (rounded up to 7). A student getting 7 or more of the 10 items correct would be qualified for the program.

TABLE 3.1 Average Item Difficulties of Seven Judges

Item Number	Average Difficulty
1	.73
2	.65
3	.90
4	.65
5	.45
6	.55
7	.60
8	.58
9	.75
10	.78
Total	6.64

The foregoing example is for an Angoff-type procedure. There may be minor variations to this procedure, depending on the application, but the process would be basically the same.

Development of Criterion-Referenced Tests

The method for developing a test to be used to report criterion-referenced scores is slightly different from the development of a test that will be used to report norm-referenced scores. The initial step in either case, however, is the same—the subject area to be assessed must be specified. It is at the item level that the difference between the two types of tests and their methods of score reporting becomes clear. Let us assume that a test developer has specified the content area and has painstakingly written 100 test items to measure that content area that are all virtually perfect in form. For a criterion-referenced test, the direct link of each item to specific skills to be assessed is the cornerstone of item development. For each skill, there may be four or more items developed so that inferences concerning mastery of the skill can be made. For the norm-referenced test, the items are developed to represent a broader range of the content domain. There may be only a single item assessing a particular skill, but the entire range of the domain will be represented.

These 100 items are then tried out or "piloted" with a group of people with characteristics similar to the ones who will eventually take the test. From the pilot, it is determined that all the people answered Question 88 correctly, and nobody answered Question 15 correctly. If the test is being developed for reporting norm-referenced scores, then neither of these items will be useful—they do not separate students or show differences in students' achievement. Consequently, these items will not be included in the test. If, on the other hand, the test is being developed to yield criterion-referenced scores and these items measure skills that the test developer wants students to know, then the items are appropriate and may still be included in the test. In essence, a norm-referenced test developer only selects items that separate test takers and deletes items that do not, even if the item measures an important concept. On the other hand, a criterion-referenced test is composed of items that measure the entire specified content domain, even if all of the test takers know or do not know the answer.

Let us return to the example of the driver's license test. When that test is being developed, the reason for including a particular item is based on the knowledge assessed by that item. If the knowledge being assessed is critical to inferring that the applicant is a safe driver, then the item will be included on the test. The state wants to assure itself that the applicant knows that information, and it is hoped everyone will answer the item correctly. If the test were a norm-referenced test, the inclusion of an item would be based on the ability of the item to differentiate applicants. There would be some items on the test that only a very few would people answer correctly and other items that only the least qualified would get wrong. In this manner, the state could identify the top and bottom scorers of the group taking the test. Because the purpose of a criterion-referenced test is to assess an individual's particular knowledge of a subject area, items that measure that knowledge are important and are included on the test.

The Need for Standardization

It is important to remember that standardization is just as important for criterion-referenced tests as it is for norm-referenced tests. If crucial decisions are going to be made about individual students based on any test result, the fact that all students are treated essentially the same is of great concern. This is true even in an individual classroom. Consider the situation where a teacher is giving a test to diagnose reading skills to plan an instructional program for a class. If the test is given to one student under one set of conditions and is given to another student under a different set of conditions (e.g., Student A is given 10 minutes to read a passage but Student B is given 30 minutes), are the results interpretable in the same fashion for both students? If both students answered 75% of the items about the passage correctly, does that score mean the same thing for each student? Consequently, is the planning going to reflect the same needs for each student? To do the job the teacher needs to do, the meaning of the test results should be comparable for all students. This comparability is partially addressed through standardizing the administration of the test.

Comparability is further addressed in the scoring of the tests. Standardization of scoring means that all tests are scored the same way. If, for example, a teacher allows penmanship to influence the content grade on an essay, then the content scores for all students are not comparable. The students with better penmanship will score higher, even if the content is the same. Penmanship may be scored, but it should be separated from the content knowledge score. The standardization of scoring assures that each student's score will be interpreted in the same way. The score should reflect as accurately as possible the student's knowledge of the content area.

Almost without exception, an effort should be made to assure standardization for all assessments. Even though teachers do not need to develop manuals for administering their own tests or written directions such as those produced by test publishers, teachers should make an effort to assure that the test administration is the same for all students and the scoring is as standardized as possible. States that have implemented writing assessments have invested considerable time and effort to develop the scoring rubrics for these assessments. These scoring rubrics guide the scoring of the students' writing and assure the validity of the tests themselves. Classroom teachers may do the same thing for their assessments. For any performance assessment, such as a writing test, the teacher should write down the elements to be used in scoring the papers. Each element should be checked the same way for every student. A lack of supporting detail on an essay should result in the same point deduction for all students. Also, it is often helpful to score the tests on an element-by-element or question-by-question basis. That is, score all tests on Question 1, and then score all tests on Question 2. This helps assure consistency of scoring. Applying the same standard to every paper will yield results that are comparable.

Advantages of Criterion-Referenced Tests

Usually, the purpose of a criterion-referenced test in a school is to evaluate the level of knowledge of a student compared to some specified level of knowledge. This might be based on a pass/fail decision or to classify the student according to some number of achievement levels.

One obvious and major advantage of a criterion-referenced test is the direct link to the instructional program. The items for such a test are selected to measure those areas the teacher or administrator believes are important for the student to have learned. The results of the criterion-referenced test are tied to the individual and/or schools and districts and are in terms of knowledge of the content domain assessed.

Criterion-referenced tests should be used when specific information concerning the level of knowledge of the student is what is needed. They are used to certify a minimum level of knowledge (competency tests fall into this category) or any specified level of knowledge using achievement levels. They may be used for promotion and graduation requirements. In settings other than education, they are used to certify physicians, dentists, hairstylists, and other professionals. Anytime the need is to know the level of knowledge of the test taker, the test to use is a criterion-referenced test.

Disadvantages of Criterion-Referenced Tests

In a very general sense, the disadvantage of a criterion-referenced test is the advantage of a norm-referenced test. A criterion-referenced test will not provide the national comparisons of performance that are reported for norm-referenced tests. If the school wants to award a faculty scholarship to a deserving student, the use of a criterion-referenced test to identify the student with the highest achievement may well result in a large number of students with the same high score. This will not assist the selection committee. The committee should use a test that will separate or identify differences in achievement among students in the school. This is a job for a norm-referenced test.

A potential disadvantage of criterion-referenced tests is the possibility that they will lead to a narrowing of the curriculum, teaching of the test, and measurement-driven instruction. Although these things could happen, they are not inherent in a criterion-referenced test. If the test is developed as has been described earlier in this chapter, the test will represent the curriculum, and therefore teaching to the test would not be a disadvantage.

Summary

A criterion-referenced test is a test that provides scores that relate test performance to some specified level of knowledge. A criterion-referenced test is used to determine what a student knows or does not know. It is directly linked to the instructional program and provides valuable information to the teacher and administrator. It is less useful in comparing an individual's performance to the performance of others. A criterion-referenced test may employ a single cut score or multiple cut scores, yielding multiple achievement levels.

Alternative
Assessment Strategies

In this chapter, we explore the area of alternative assessments. They are also referred to as "authentic assessments" or "performance assessments." The first thing one should know about alternative assessments is that they may be considered a special case of criterion-referenced tests. They are usually designed to provide information about a student's level of knowledge in some specific subject area. Recent editions of nationally norm-referenced tests have included alternative assessments (e.g., writing assessments) as part of the assessment battery so that it is possible to create these tests and generate norm-referenced scores, but this is not usually the case. Therefore, we will consider them a special case of a criterion-referenced test, serving the same purpose as criterion-referenced tests with all the attendant advantages and disadvantages.

In another sense, it seems reasonable to ask Why are these assessments called alternative assessments? and What is it they are an alternative to? Before the era of large-scale assessments using multiple-choice items, the tests used by most teachers were essays, oral presentations, portfolios, and other types of performance assessments. The student had to demonstrate to the teacher the knowledge being assessed. The development of standardized multiple-choice tests in the early part of this century replaced these traditional methods of assessment in many situations. The new multiple-choice tests could be administered to great numbers of people with relative ease, and the tests could be scored by machine. These multiple-choice tests became the standard method of assessment for large-scale applications (e.g., college entrance, high school graduation, statewide assessments). We now have come to the point where we are looking back to the assessments used extensively by individual teachers in one-room schoolhouses as possible alternatives to the multiple-choice tests.

In the debate over alternative assessments, the question being asked is not whether these tests are good assessment devices, but rather whether these tests can be used in large-scale applications with the same objectivity and understandability as multiple-choice tests. Whenever a test requires a student to demonstrate knowledge as part of the assessment, it presents a set of unique challenges to the teacher or administrator. For example, if one desires to use a writing assessment to determine whether students are able to write, as opposed to merely asking them multiple-choice questions about the writing process, certain conditions must change. The testing situation usually will be longer and require more effort by the student. The most obvious change, however, is in scoring. If essays are being read by a group of readers (one person could not read 50,000 essays for a single grade in a statewide assessment), are these people all grading the same way? The question of objective scoring is a real concern to many consumers of test data, from teachers and principals to parents and students. They all want the tests to be as fair as possible. These issues are concerned with the application of the alternative assessments in a large-scale context, not whether the tests themselves are useful for assessing student learning. Many, if not all, of the alternative assessments are currently being used on a regular basis by teachers in classrooms nationwide as a part of instructional strategies.

There are different types of alternative assessments that educators should become familiar with as their inclusion in statewide testing programs is debated. Each of these types of tests enjoys special advantages and is especially suited to certain situations. It should be kept in mind that these tests are well proven in the classroom and should be a valuable tool in the teacher's testing toolbox.

Types of Alternative Assessments

Alternative assessments generally require a student to demonstrate the knowledge being assessed. This demonstration may take the form of an essay, exhibition, portfolio, or other type of assessment, but they all require more than simply marking a correct answer on an answer sheet. The following is a list of some of the more popular types of alternative assessments.

1. Constructed-response items
2. Essays
3. Performance tasks
4. Exhibitions and demonstrations
5. Portfolios
6. Classroom presentations and oral discourse

There are other forms of alternative assessments, but the above list is inclusive of the main forms being discussed in the debate over the use of alternative assessments. It also should be noted that the list is not mutually exclusive. That is, some alternative assessments could fit into more than one of the categories. The remainder of this chapter gives a brief description of the various types of alternative assessments and provides an indication of their strengths and weaknesses.

Constructed-Response Items

Constructed-response items are not really a type of assessment, but they are an alternative to traditional multiple-choice items. These items require students to provide their own answers to a stated problem rather than select the correct answer from a given set of options. A constructed-response item may have one correct answer or it may be more open ended, allowing a range of correct responses. The form may vary from filling in a blank or writing a short answer to drawing a graph or diagram or writing out all the steps in a geometric proof. The key element is for a student to produce the answer to the question rather than select the answer from a list of possible answers.

Essays

An essay is a writing sample used to assess student understanding and may be used to evaluate how well students can analyze and synthesize information. It is used to assess a student's understanding of a subject through a written description, analysis, explanation, or summary. Answering an essay question requires critical thinking, analysis, and synthesis. Essays effectively assess the depth of student knowledge in a limited content area, whereas multiple-choice tests are used to assess a broad range of knowledge at a less substantial level.

Performance Tasks

A performance task is a demonstration of a student's competence in performing an activity. It may require the student to produce a piece of writing, solve mathematically or scientifically complex problems, or complete a science experiment. Students are provided the opportunity to apply knowledge, skills, and experience to complete real or simulated workplace tasks. Students are required to gather information, interpret it, and link it to what is known; diagnose problem situations; develop possible alternatives or solutions to the problem or task; implement a course of action; and follow up their work. The performance task is then judged against established criteria.

Achievement objectives that do not lend themselves to paper-and-pencil tests may be more appropriately assessed by having students actually demonstrate their competence. For example, a performance task is not only appropriate but necessary to license people to drive cars. The assurance that an applicant has the requisite knowledge of driving rules and laws is not sufficient. The applicant must actually drive a car and perform common driving maneuvers to be issued a driver's license. In the classroom, having students determine the amount of carpet needed to cover the floor by calculating the total square footage is a performance task. This type of assessment allows for student variation in approaching the problem and often may allow for multiple correct answers. To some extent, the process of problem solving may be as important as the ultimate answer in the assessment.

Exhibitions and Demonstrations

An exhibition or demonstration is used to allow students to show their mastery of a skill or competence by requiring the student to demonstrate that skill or competence. It may be interdisciplinary and require student initiative and creativity, it may be in the form of a competition between individual students or groups, or it may be a collaborative project that students work on over time. An exhibition may be a musical performance, a dramatic presentation, a sports event, a spelling contest, a math tournament, or other similar activity.

Portfolios

A portfolio is a purposeful collection of samples of a student's work that is selective, reflective, and collaborative and demonstrates the range and depth of a student's achievement, competencies, and skills over time and across a variety of contexts. Fischer and King (1995) identify the most common types of portfolios as the working portfolio, the showcase portfolio, and the record-keeping portfolio. Portfolios are a visual presentation of a student's accomplishments, capabilities, strengths, weaknesses, and progress during their school years. They provide a glimpse of where the student has been and where the student is going. Portfolios may serve different purposes during the year but should reflect effort and growth. Depending on the type of portfolio, it may contain pieces worked on by the student during the entire year and include the draft outline, the first draft, and the final product. It might also contain a piece produced at one time to reflect learning status at that time. The portfolio might contain a writing sample that was produced "on demand" concerning a single subject as well as documents that reflect the more traditional prewriting, editing, and final drafts. The subjects that may be included in a portfolio are limited only by the design of the developer.

Classroom Presentations and Oral Discourse

It is common practice today for graduate students to be tested with oral defenses of theses and dissertations. Oral discourse can also be used to assess young children when it is inappropriate to test with paper and pencil. Oral presentations require students to verbalize their knowledge and organize thoughts in a way different from other testing situations. Certain areas are naturally aligned with this type of assessment, for example, foreign languages. Requiring a student to speak allows for the assessment of fluency in the language. However, this type of assessment is not limited to measuring foreign language knowledge. Asking children to make speeches in an English class or participate in organized debates are other examples of assessment using oral discourse.

The Need for Standardization: Objectivity in Scoring

The major criticism leveled at alternative assessments is that they are often not standardized. It is felt that they are more subjective and therefore less desirable than the more traditional multiple-choice tests. If the score received by a student is a function of the person grading the assessment and not a reflection of the knowledge presented, then the test is of no value. There are a number of things that can be done to standardize the scoring procedures and, therefore, increase the objectivity of the scoring for alternative assessments. By objectivity, we mean that different scorers would give essentially the same grade to an individual's test. Obviously, a machine-scored, multiple-choice test is highly objective. That is, the machine will score all papers the same way. In scoring a classroom presentation or judging the contents of a portfolio, it is not as obvious how the scoring can be made to be objective.

A number of methods are available for scoring alternative assessments that will increase the objectivity of the scoring process.

The cornerstone of each of these procedures is the training of graders in how to use the methods. As a consequence, the most important components in scoring alternative assessments are training scorers to use the method selected and monitoring the actual scoring to assure consistency within individual judges and among all judges. The most common method of scoring alternative assessments is through scoring rubrics. A scoring rubric defines the various levels of performance and the elements required within each level. Scorers use the rubric to compare a student's performance to these detailed definitions of performance. For performance assessments, often the rubric is identified by four to six score points or achievement levels as discussed earlier. McColskey and O'Sullivan (1995) listed the following rubrics that are used to evaluate student performance on alternative assessments.

1. Point system: A point system assigns points for certain features of a student's response. Open-ended questions are often scored with this approach because points can reflect partial as well as full credit for a response.

2. Checklists: A checklist can be used to indicate that a student has effectively completed the steps involved in a performance task or demonstration. Checklists may be applied to written work or observable behavior.

3. Analytic rating scales: Rating scales describe performance along a continuum. Analytic rating scales are used to describe a product or performance on multiple dimensions. For example, in a writing task, the dimensions or criteria that might be rated are organization, mechanics, and creativity. Each important dimension of the task performance is rated on a 2- (e.g., *acceptable, not acceptable*) or more (e.g., *not adequate, partially satisfactory, satisfactory, exemplary*) point scale.

4. Focused holistic rating scales: Focused holistic ratings consider all the scoring criteria simultaneously, rather than assigning separate scores for each important aspect of task performance, and results in a single summary grade or rating. This approach may be most appropriate when the purpose is to provide students with an overall index of their performance on a task or product.

5. Holistic scoring: With this type of scoring, definitions are provided and model responses are selected that represent numbers on the scale to be used. Student responses are compared to the definitions and model responses and given a number corresponding to the model response they are most like.

Advantages of Alternative Assessments

Because alternative assessments are designed to have students do or demonstrate what they know, they provide a direct link for an inference concerning what they have learned. The influence of guessing that is present in any multiple-choice assessment is eliminated, and thus, potentially more accurate inferences are possible. This assumes, however, that the performance of the student is an accurate reflection of what the student actually knows or can do. Most teachers would admit to being more comfortable making statements about student learning if they have actually seen the student engage in activities requiring that learning. Alternative assessments look like they are actual demonstrations of student learning and not a poor substitute for estimating student learning.

Disadvantages of Alternative Assessments

One of the major disadvantages of alternative assessments is the time required to administer and score them. To have students demonstrate a skill or to maintain 20-25 student portfolios requires much more time than giving a paper-and-pencil test over the contents of a chapter. Scoring alternative assessments requires even more time.

To the extent that the evaluation (scoring) of the alternative assessment does not reflect the true learning of the student, the assessment becomes less useful. The problem is one of assuring objectivity in scoring and the standardization of scoring procedures. It is difficult to assure that all scorers are using the same standard to judge performance. A greater emphasis is placed on training and monitoring of the scoring process than in other forms of assessment.

Summary

Alternative assessments are familiar to teachers who use many of the techniques in the classroom. They involve constructed-response items, essay tests, portfolios, performance tasks, exhibitions or demonstrations, and oral presentations. They are being used with ever-increasing frequency in large-scale assessments. Alternative assessments do, however, present a set of unique problems for large-scale assessments. Even though they closely represent what they attempt to assess, the standardization needed for valid scoring requires training and time. This greatly increases the cost of the assessments for large-scale applications. Within the classroom, the use of alternative assessments offers the teacher more information about student learning than would be obtained from traditional multiple-choice tests. They should be considered one possible assessment tool in the testing toolbox of teachers.

Using Assessment Results
to Improve Schools

The common goal of educators, parents, and policymakers is to improve the education of students. Each of these groups sees tests and assessment as playing a role in this endeavor. However, educators and policymakers see assessment as playing different roles. Educators see assessment as providing information for making instructional decisions. Policymakers see assessment as providing information for accountability decisions. The problem is that the competing types of decisions being made by educators and policymakers may best be supported by different types of assessments: criterion referenced and norm referenced. Educators want to know if curriculum goals are being met (criterion referenced), whereas policymakers find comparisons most enlightening (norm referenced).

The solution to this dilemma of whether to use nationally standardized norm-referenced tests or criterion-referenced tests may best be solved by developing a comprehensive assessment program that uses a combination of norm-referenced and criterion-referenced assessments to gain the advantages of both. Implementing a well-designed, comprehensive assessment program and keeping it in place over a period of time maximizes its usefulness. All assessment programs, whether based on norm-referenced tests, criterion-referenced tests, or some combination, yield the most beneficial results when they are left in place over a period of time and outcomes are interpreted longitudinally. All of these assessment approaches yield data that can be used to estimate improvement.

The major danger associated with any assessment program is that the tests become the master of the curriculum. A curriculum should be established and the assessments should be chosen that best reflect that curriculum. The choice of a test, particularly a general, nationally standardized norm-referenced test, should not dictate the curriculum, as is often the case when it is the primary basis of the assessment program. If assessments are selected that do not reflect the curriculum, the curriculum will change over time to reflect the assessments. The validity of any assessment program is determined by how well the assessments match the curriculum. Because curricula are broad based but include components unique to an individual state, a combination of nationally standardized norm-referenced tests and state-based criterion-referenced tests should be used for a balanced and effective statewide assessment program, and performance assessments may be included.

Steps for Developing an Ideal Assessment Program

An ideal assessment program, whether at the state, system, or school level, can be developed in six steps. The six steps also provide a summary of the content of this book. The six steps are as follows:

1. *Establish the purpose of assessment.* The first step is to define the purpose or purposes of the assessment. Broad purposes include educational improvement and accountability. More specific purposes, such as the monitoring of the curriculum or the evaluation of a specific program, are also appropriate. The validity of the tests used in the assessment cannot be determined unless clear purposes are established (see chapter 1).

2. *Define the content domain.* The second step involves defining the content domain or the specific areas of the curriculum to be assessed. The process needed to implement a criterion-referenced test or a norm-referenced test is dependent on completely specifying what it is that the student should know or be able to do. The domain of interest (e.g., U.S. history from 1860 until 1995, Algebra 1, reading comprehension) must be clearly specified. The objectives within the domain must be identified and the types of items best suited to measure the knowledge established. The content domain must be defined with enough specificity to allow the content validity of the test(s) to be determined.

3. *Develop assessment-planning matrices.* The first-level planning matrix would be appropriate for districts or higher level agencies developing an assessment program. This matrix would indicate the types of tests to be given, the grades to be tested, and the general content areas to be assessed. The second-level planning matrix is a table that includes the levels or grades being assessed across the columns and the content in the rows. This provides a basis for judging the content validity of the test or tests being used. The first step in developing an assessment-planning matrix is to make a list of the content to be covered. Second, place the grades (or levels) to be covered in the columns. The third step is to determine the emphasis to be placed on the content described in each line by dividing 100% among the items of content. Finally, the percentage assigned to each content line is divided among the grades or levels covered.

Suppose that a school instituted a whole language program for language arts in Grades 1-3. Figure 5.1 illustrates a second-level assessment-planning matrix.

4. *Select tests and determine timing.* Using the assessment-planning matrix and the purposes of the tests, select valid measures that cover the matrix to the maximum extent. It is also important to consider the timing of the assessments. Should they be done in the early fall, late spring, both, or some other time? Again, the purpose of the assessment helps determine this. If the purpose is to assist teachers in developing learning plans for individual students,

Content	Grade			Emphasis
	1	2	3	
Oral Language Development	10%	5%	5%	20%
Knowledge Construction	5%	5%	10%	20%
Reading Comprehension	5%	7%	8%	20%
Writing Communication	4%	6%	10%	20%
Social Process Skills	4%	3%	3%	10%
Risk Tolerance	3%	3%	4%	10%

Figure 5.1. Assessment-Planning Matrix for Whole Language Example

early fall may be most appropriate. If, on the other hand, the purpose is primarily for accountability, late spring may be most appropriate. If the primary purpose is to evaluate a specific program, early fall and late spring (pre- and post-) testing may be most appropriate. At the same time, the amount of time to be devoted to testing should be considered. If the school system has 180 days per year, a week of testing (5 days) in the fall and a week of testing (5 days) in the spring would account for over 5% of the total instructional time available. In most cases, this would be the maximum testing time that should be considered. This rule of thumb should be tempered by many factors such as the age of the students, the purposes of the test (instructional vs. accountability), and the scheduling of the tests (on consecutive days or spread out).

The assessment-planning matrix is not only useful for selecting valid measures, it is very useful for determining the weighting of multiple assessments, especially if one or more of those assessments is a performance assessment. For example, how do you determine the relative weights of a writing assessment and set of multiple-choice items for an overall language arts score? This can be done by determining the cells covered in the assessment-planning matrix by each type of assessment and adding up the percentages in these cells.

5. *Implement the assessment.* Implementation should include the training of the proctors and administrators, establishing security of the tests, and planning the logistics of testing. Training of the proctors and administrators should not be minimized. As was shown with Regina's example in Chapter 2, minor variations from the prescribed standardized conditions can result in dramatic changes in the interpretations of the results. Security issues should be addressed and, at a minimum, should include a definite policy on test security (preferably a board policy) as well as the signing of security agreements by anyone who handles the tests. It is best to have the tests in the schools a minimum amount of time.

6. *Use the results.* If specific purposes for the testing were defined as suggested in Step 1, the use of the results will already be clear. It is important for those involved to know beforehand how the results are interpreted and how they will be used. Just placing the test results in a drawer is a waste of money, student instructional time, and teacher time. The results are most useful when viewed over the long term. Achievement trends are an important element in an effective use plan.

Improving the Efficiency of Assessment

There are several measures that can be implemented to improve the efficiency of the assessment process. The basic principle behind these measures is the reduction of testing time for students. The measures range from potentially complex methods that may require professional assistance to the implementation of simple procedures requiring only a little forethought. It should be kept in mind that time not used for testing could be used for instruction, and increased instructional time is the one activity that research has been able to link to increased achievement.

The first approach to improving the efficiency of assessment is to determine if each test used in the assessment is necessary. A test is necessary if it addresses a purpose of the assessment that cannot be measured in a more efficient manner. Judging the necessity of a test assumes that the purposes of the assessment program have been delineated. This also requires that alternative methods of meeting the purpose have been considered. The key element for improving the efficiency of assessment is the clear delineation of its purposes.

Once tests to be included in the assessment program have been determined, other efficiencies can be effected by reducing the number of times the tests are given. It is erroneous to assume that every test must be given to every student every year. First, look for obvious ways to reduce testing. For example, suppose that a program (like Title 1) requires pre- and posttests each year to evaluate the outcomes of the program. Many educators assume this to mean that they must pretest in September and posttest in May. However, if proper student records are kept and students can be matched year to year, the May testing from the previous year can serve as the pretest for the present year, reducing the testing time by half.

Such a system requires the ability to easily match the scores of students from one year to the next. Although records can be matched using names, this is not very efficient for a number of reasons. One reason is that students often list their names differently. For example, one student may list his name as John Smith, Johnny Smith, and John K. Smith for different testings. Furthermore, there may be more than one John Smith. It is an effective practice to use identification numbers such as social security numbers on test forms. These are unique and allow the matching of scores using a computer, a process that is very efficient.

A more sophisticated system for reducing the testing time required for individual students is a process referred to as matrix sampling. Simply, matrix sampling is a process in which each student is given only a portion of the test each year. Matrix sampling can be implemented at several levels. The simplest approach is to select different tests to be given at the different grade levels. Thus all areas of the curriculum can be assessed, but individual students only take those tests assigned to their grade. This is illustrated through an example in the next section.

More complicated applications can be implemented, such as having the students from the same group (such as a grade) take different subtests or items. Using this approach, no single student takes the entire set of tests, but results are available from all the tests because all of the tests are given to some students. The advantage of this approach is the reduction of testing time for individual students and for test administrators. The disadvantage is that individual students do not get scores. Thus this approach is primarily useful for accountability purposes or for evaluating programs. The complications in scoring and interpreting scores for this type of matrix sampling suggests that measurement specialists should be consulted before it is applied.

The bottom line in improving the efficiency of assessment is to minimize the amount of testing. This is done by selecting only the tests that are needed to address the purposes of the assessment program and applying them in as efficient a manner as possible. Great effort should be made to have teachers realize that assessments are a critical part of the instructional program.

An Example

The first step in establishing an assessment program is to determine the purpose or purposes for giving the assessment. For this example, let us assume that the sponsoring agency for the assessment program is a large school district, having as many as 50 schools throughout a large geographical area. The local board of education has committed to improve student learning throughout the district and wants to assure the general public that their trust in the elected board is warranted. At the same time, the board wants to provide information to teachers and school administrators concerning teaching and learning. Finally, the state's legislature has mandated that all students who graduate from high school must demonstrate the acquisition of minimum skills in reading, language, and mathematics. These, then, define three separate purposes for an assessment program. It is unlikely that one test could satisfy all three purposes; therefore, different tests will be used to meet the needs of the board.

Establish the Purpose of the Assessment

The first purpose is an accountability purpose. From the perspective of the district, this represents questions such as How are the students of this district achieving compared to other students throughout the state and with students in the nation? If the need is for norm-referenced scores (both within the state and within the nation), then the test needed is a nationally standardized norm-referenced achievement test.

The second purpose for the assessment program expressed by the board is to provide information to teachers and administrators about student learning. Because students usually are taught from a district-approved curriculum or course of study, the assessment should measure student learning of that curriculum. It is implied in such a purpose that some level of acceptability of achievement will be specified. That is, it can be assumed that a cut score or cut scores will be established on these assessments. The need is for a criterion-referenced score, and the test needed is a criterion-referenced test designed to assess the district's curriculum.

The third purpose, imposed by the state legislature, is to assure the acquisition of minimum skills as a precondition for receiving a high school diploma. This assessment would also be a criterion-referenced test, but one that focuses on minimum skills.

Define the Content Domain

The next step in developing an assessment program is to determine which content will be assessed in which grades. The state legislature has mandated that areas of reading, mathematics, and language be assessed with the criterion-referenced graduation examination. For this example, we will assume that the board has decided to assess only reading comprehension and mathematics using norm-referenced tests. Furthermore, they decided to assess writing, mathematics, science, and social studies from their courses of study.

Even though the subject areas to be assessed have now been determined, the specific objectives from within those content domains must be selected. This selection of specific objectives to be tested is usually accomplished by teachers who know the content and can decide which are the important objectives to be assessed. It is important to remember that no test can assess all learning objectives, so the selection of the objectives to be assessed is critical to the inference about the achievement of the entire content domain. The definition of the specific objectives allows for the content validity of the test to be evaluated. That is, are the items on the test measuring the content objectives that they were intended to measure? Unless the content domain is defined with enough specificity, the content validity of the test cannot be determined.

Develop an Assessment-Planning Matrix

The assessment-planning matrix displays the results of decisions made concerning the subjects and grades to be assessed. These decisions are often affected by factors other than the stated purposes for the assessment program such as cost. For our example, we will discuss two levels of planning matrices. The first level would indicate the subject area by type of test to be assessed in which grades. The second level would indicate the within-subject area emphasis for each grade (Figure 5.1 is an example of this level).

Using all the resources available to it, the local board of education decides to assess student learning relative to the national norming group in Grades 4, 6, and 8. These tests will yield student performance in terms of percentile ranks and stanines. They can be used to compare the performance of the district's students with students from the norming group. This test will meet the first purpose that the board had specified.

The board also decides, based on factors such as cost and testing burden, to assess writing in Grades 5, 7, and 10; science in Grades 5, 7, and 9; social studies in Grades 6 and 8; and mathematics in Grade 7 and at the high school level using end-of-course tests in algebra and geometry. Each of these tests would be criterion-referenced tests based on the district's courses of study in those areas.

Type of Test (Score Type) and Subject	Grade								
	4	5	6	7	8	9	10	11	12
Nationally Norm-Referenced (Percentiles, Stanines)									
Reading Comprehension	✓		✓		✓				
Mathematics	✓		✓		✓				
Criterion-Referenced Tests (Achievement Levels)									
Writing		✓		✓			✓		
Mathematics				✓		✓	✓		
Science		✓		✓		✓			
Social Studies			✓		✓				
High School Graduation Examination (Pass/Fail)									
Reading								✓	✓
Language								✓	✓
Mathematics								✓	✓

Figure 5.2. First-Level Planning Matrix for the District

Figure 5.2 represents the first-level planning matrix for the district. It shows the results of the decisions of the board concerning which subjects and which grades will be tested. It indicates the type of test to be used and includes the legislatively mandated graduation test.

Select the Tests and Determine Timing

The selection of the norm-referenced test to be used by the district should be decided based on the degree to which the test matches the curriculum being taught in the district. Commercially published tests are based on the general concepts of curriculum from a broad segment of the country. They are developed so that, it is hoped, they will be useful in many schools, districts, and states. There are variations in content coverage between the various published norm-referenced tests, and the district should use teachers and administrators to evaluate all possible tests and select the one with the best match to the content that is taught and the methods used to teach it in the district.

The criterion-referenced tests in writing, mathematics, science, and social studies will have to be developed by the district unless there are commercially available assessments that completely match what the district teachers want to test. Again, the best resource for the district to use in developing or selecting these tests are the teachers in the district. If items are to be developed by the district, the use of teachers as item writers and on bias committees to review items will help assure reliable and valid items. The training required for teachers to become item writers is beyond the scope of this book but is a major component in the development process.

Decisions about the scoring rubric for the writing assessment must be made by the district and training provided to all district teachers about the rubric. Another decision concerns when to test the students. The board decides to focus assessment on the end of the year and elects to use spring testing for all tests except the graduation examination, which is given in the fall of the junior year.

Implement the Assessment Program

The implementation of a successful assessment program requires more than just giving the test. In our example, the board has begun a comprehensive testing program that will require training of test administrators and proctors. It also requires professional development for all teachers and administrators to understand the purposes and anticipated uses for the test data. The board should adopt a policy concerning test security and require all persons who will have contact with the tests to sign a test security agreement. The board must also set policy concerning storage and transport of the tests to schools. As was recommended earlier, it is best to have the tests in the schools for a minimum amount of time. This is especially true for high-stakes tests such as the graduation test.

Use the Results

This may be the most important aspect of the assessment program. The results must be used to accomplish the purposes for which the test was given. For the norm-referenced test, the board should decide on how test scores will be reported to the public. Will they produce a "report card" for each school or use other methods of communicating to the public? The way the results are reported will greatly affect the public's understanding of the assessment program. Care should be taken to present information in such a way as to avoid misinterpretation.

For the criterion-referenced assessments, the reporting of student performance in terms of achievement levels, with specific definitions of what the levels mean in terms of student performance, will help avoid misinterpretation of those data. For example, if the writing assessments were reported in four levels and the definitions of these levels indicate, in noneducation jargon, how well the student can write, the public will gain an understanding of the achievement of students. Without national comparisons, there appears to be a basic distrust of other scores. The education of the public is critical to forming the alliances often necessary to improve student achievement.

The measurement of knowledge gained by students who were exposed to the district courses of study would require that the data generated from those tests be usable by teachers to plan instruction and by administrators to evaluate the educational programs within the schools. The use of achievement levels, as well as indicators of the percentage of students at those achievement levels, coupled with objective level scoring, will provide the information needed by teachers and administrators to improve teaching and learning.

School Testing Programs

Even with all the testing being imposed on local schools and teachers (not to mention students) by state governments, the need for a balanced assessment program still would exist at the school level. The six-step process for implementing an ideal assessment program can also be implemented at the school level. Teachers should strive to integrate assessments into their instructional programs. It is unfortunate that some teachers bemoan the time spent testing as time taken away from instruction. The assessment program should be a part of the instructional program. It should provide information to the teacher to modify or enhance the instruction occurring in the classroom, identify student strengths and weaknesses, or be used as part of the formative evaluation of students. One major problem with this recommendation is that most teachers receive little or no training in assessment as they prepare for life in the classroom. Therefore, a great need exists to provide teachers with the inservice training needed to make them better creators of tests and users of test results.

Sharing Results

Once a test is given, who should have access to the results? This is a question that has concerned educators since testing began in our schools. The question should also be rephrased as Who should not have access to the results? The answers to these questions need to be considered separately for individual-score results and group or aggregated results.

Let us first address who should have access to individual-score results. Obviously, the student or the student's parents or guardians should have access. In fact, this is a matter of federal law (Federal Family Education Rights and Privacy Act of 1974). This law requires that students and/or their parents or guardians have access to test scores on request. This requirement imposes a professional responsibility on school systems to provide assistance in the proper interpretation of these test scores. Thus counselors and other school personnel must have access to student test scores as well as the teachers. Federal law also restricts those who should have access to individual scores (Buckley Amendment of the Federal Family Educational Rights and Privacy Act of 1974). Access by any other agency or individual (other than by court order) can only be given by the student or the student's parent or guardian in writing.

Access to grouped or aggregated data in which individual students' scores cannot be determined is another matter. These results can be made available to all educators in the system, the board of education, newspapers, and the general public. Such access again carries with it a professional responsibility to provide appropriate interpretations.

Final Thoughts

Assessment is an awesome responsibility for administrators and teachers. It has the ability to improve education through its appropriate use in the teaching-learning process. It is also a primary means of communicating the effectiveness of our schools to parents, the general public, and politicians. On the other hand, assessment can serve as a destructive force if it is not used and interpreted properly, wasting student instructional time and providing misleading information to parents, the general public, and boards of education.

If assessment is to be a positive force in education, it must be implemented properly. It cannot be used to merely sort students or to criticize education. Its goal must be to improve education. Rather than "teach the test," we must "test what we teach." In doing so, teaching the test in a broad sense (content, not items) is appropriate. In the end, assessment can improve both the teaching and learning process and provide a level of accountability if it is done properly.

Annotated Bibliography
and References

Brandt, R. S. (Ed.). (1994). Reporting what students are learning [Special issue]. *Educational Leadership, 52*(2).

This special issue provides an excellent, in-depth look at reporting student achievement from several perspectives. Not only does it cover the usual teacher and administrator perspectives, but it also considers reporting of achievement from the viewpoints of students, parents, and the general public. The authors range from a student to leaders in the field of measurement.

Fischer, C. F., & King, R. M. (1995). *Authentic assessment: A guide to implementation.* Thousand Oaks, CA: Corwin.

This is an excellent, up-to-date resource for teachers who want or need to implement authentic assessment in their classrooms. It includes easy-to-understand definitions and provides the steps needed to get started using authentic assessment. There are chapters addressing the needs of administrators and how to involve students, parents, and the community in the learning process.

Hymes, D. L., Chafin, A. E., & Gonder, P. (1991). *The changing face of testing and assessment: Problems and solutions.* Arlington, VA: American Association of School Administrators.

This Critical Issues Report from AASA provides background information and examples of current practice, including "report cards" and sample scoring rubrics for writing and mathematics. It addresses criteria for evaluating assessment systems. This report provides a summary of the evolution of testing in education over the past 100 years and includes issues not addressed in many other documents, such as the standards for teacher competence in the educational assessment of students.

Jorgensen, M. (1986). *Basic differences between norm-referenced and criterion-referenced tests.* Atlanta, GA: Southern Regional Education Board.

This little 19-page pamphlet provides a concise overview of the basic differences between the two types of tests. It also includes some guidelines for selecting a test and the number of items that might be needed for a particular purpose. The section on criterion-referenced tests focuses only on single cut-score situations, but this should not limit its usefulness in learning to understand the differences in the two types of tests.

Linn, R. L. (Ed.). (1989). *Educational measurement* (3rd ed.). New York: Macmillan.

This third edition of a classic in the measurement field brings together ideas from current leaders in the measurement field. Although it is somewhat technical in nature, it covers the theory, processes, and applications of measurement. For the most part, it is up to date. However, it does not address performance assessment in any detail.

Livingston, S. A., & Zieky, M. J. (1982). *Passing scores: A manual for setting standards of educational and occupational tests.* Princeton, NJ: Educational Testing Service.

This small book is a primer for setting cut scores. If a school system were to undertake the setting of their own cut scores, this would be a very useful reference. It covers a number of methods for making judgments about test items and for making judgments about test takers.

Lyman, H. B. (1991). *Test scores and what they mean* (5th ed.). Needham Heights, MA: Allyn & Bacon.

This is a very readable book on testing and measurement for teachers and administrators. It has a very useful chapter on the meaning and derivation of standard scores used in tests, and it is presented at an understandable level for most educators.

McColskey, W., & O'Sullivan, R. (1995). *How to assess student performance in science: Going beyond multiple-choice tests* (Rev. ed.). Greensboro, NC: Southeastern Regional Vision for Education.

Even though the title relates to science, this booklet presents current information on alternative assessment that is applicable to any number of subject areas. The authors address different student assessment methods in sufficient detail to allow a teacher to use the booklet as a resource guide. It provides extensive information on rubrics and grading for student-generated responses.

McLean, J. E. (1995). *Improving education through action research: A guide for administrators and teachers.* Thousand Oaks, CA: Corwin.

Assessment is of little value if it is not used. This book provides one method of using the results for improving education. It details how to use assessment results in a program of action research. Details concerning design, analysis, and interpretation of action research studies are included.

Popham, W. J. (1990). *Modern educational measurement: A practitioner's perspective* (2nd ed.). Needham Heights, MA: Allyn & Bacon.

This book is an excellent general textbook on testing and assessment. It is written in a very readable style by a noted authority on criterion-referenced assessment. In addition to the expected chapters on reliability and validity, it addresses issues such as test bias and setting performance standards. Popham also provides an entire chapter on what to look for in an educational test. Highly recommended as a general treatment of educational assessment.

Stiggins, R. J. (1994). *Student-centered classroom assessment.* New York: Macmillan.

One of the few books to specifically address the issues of assessment in the classroom. Written for teachers, this book covers both cognitive and affective assessment and has three chapters devoted to communicating about student achievement.

Tyler, R. W., & Wolf, R. M. (Eds.). (1974). *Crucial issues in testing*. Berkeley, CA: McCutchan.

Although this book is somewhat dated, it provides insights into the assessment process by many of the pioneers of the testing movement. It has a particularly good discussion of the issue of testing and minority groups. It does address early criterion-referenced testing but does not address performance assessment.

**CORWIN
PRESS**

The Corwin Press logo—a raven striding across an open book—represents the happy union of courage and learning. We are a professional-level publisher of books and journals for K–12 educators, and we are committed to creating and providing resources that embody these qualities. Corwin's motto is "Success for All Learners."